JESUS

HE IS YOUR ANSWER

JESUS

HE IS YOUR ANSWER

Walking With Jesus

EVANGELIST
JOAN PEARCE

"NOW THAT YOU HAVE ASKED JESUS INTO YOUR HEART, WHAT IS NEXT?"

Now that you have asked Jesus into your heart, it is important for you to know who you are in Christ Jesus. I want to share with you the Word of God, because the Word of God is living and powerful and it will change, transform and take you from where you are today, with problems and addictions in your life or whatever you are going through, to where Jesus wants you to be. You are probably saying, *I don't know what happened to me.* This book will explain your experience, and how you proceed from this point onward.

Why did you pray and ask Jesus into your life and what did this prayer really mean to you?

ॐ

'Therefore, if anyone is in Christ, *he is* a new creation; old things have passed away; behold, all things have become new. Now all things *are* of God, who has

reconciled us to Himself through Jesus Christ, and has given us the ministry of reconciliation, that is, that God was in Christ reconciling the world to Himself, not imputing their trespasses to them, and has committed to us the word of reconciliation.'

(2 Corinthians 5:17-19)

Let me explain to you why it is so important for you to have Jesus in your life leading you.

In the beginning, there was a war in heaven and Satan was cast out to Earth. Adam and Eve were put in the garden. The devil tempted them and convinced them to disobey God. Because of their disobedience, sin came into the whole world and the whole world changed; including the animals, and plants. Everything (all creation) was put under a curse. All human beings were born into the world with a sin nature.

Jesus came to restore us back to the original state that God intended in the beginning. His plan was to have fellowship with us. The Father sent Jesus Christ to die on a cross to be a mediator to bring us back into the fullness of fellowship with the Father, the Son (Jesus Christ) and the Holy Spirit. God wants you to know that when you pray that prayer and ask Jesus into your heart, you were taken out of the kingdom of satan and put into the kingdom of God. Now you have become a true son or daughter – child of God – and God will protect and watch over you. You need to know that Jesus is your very best friend and you want to stay focused on Jesus and know that He will take care of any problems and any needs you have.

It doesn't mean your life is going to be easy. It just means Jesus will always be there for you.

The story is told of a priest named Nicodemus who came to Jesus one night and he wanted to know how to get to heaven. Let us look at what Jesus said to him:

cରୈ

There was a man of the Pharisees named Nicodemus, a ruler of the Jews. This man came to Jesus by night and said to Him, "Rabbi, we know that You are a teacher come

from God; for no one can do these signs that You do unless God is with him." Jesus answered and said to him, "Most assuredly, I say to you, unless one is born again, he cannot see the kingdom of God." Nicodemus said to Him, "How can a man be born when he is old? Can he enter a second time into his mother's womb and be born?"

(John 3:1-4)

The man didn't understand what Jesus was saying. He was thinking in the natural, but God was saying that his spirit needed to be born again. Because of the fall of Adam, sin came into the whole world. Because of what happened in the garden, the sin nature came into all mankind. He was detached from God and now man had to be re-attached again, and the process of re-attachment is called being born again. That is just a simple way of explaining it. God wants us all to be reconnected to Him again.

⁂

Jesus answered, "Most assuredly, I say to you, unless one is born of water and the Spirit, he cannot enter the kingdom of God. That which is born of the flesh is flesh, and that which is born of the Spirit is spirit. Do not marvel that I said to you, 'You must be born again.'

(John 3:5-8)

You are an eternal being. You will never die. Your physical body will die and go to the grave. I am sure you have been to funerals. You know the body will eventually wear out and die, but God says we are eternal spirit beings. We will live forever. The question is, *"Where will we live forever?"* There are two choices: you will either be in hell or heaven. Both are real places. It is not a figment of man's imagination. They are real places. Jesus came so you don't have to go to hell. He came so you could make the right choice and go to heaven. You are going to live forever, but where? To go to heaven, your spirit must be born again. Jesus said He is the way, the truth and the life (John 14:6) and there is no other way to heaven, except through Jesus. There are a lot of voices out there telling you there are other ways. The truth is there is only one way.

ONLY THROUGH JESUS CAN YOU BE BORN AGAIN!

Satan comes to steal, kill and destroy (John 10:10). Jesus has made a way to take people to heaven and that is why you must make a choice.

CHOOSE JESUS!

Some people say to me, *"Well, why didn't He just make it so that we all automatically make the right choice and go to heaven?"*

Well, let me ask you this. If you had somebody you love, and they were a robot who was programmed to love you, and you wounded them like a little toy doll and it just said, *'I love you'* – how would you know it really loves you, because it has no choice except to say I love you? God gives us a free choice so we can choose to love Him – not because we are forced to love Him or programmed to love Him. It is a choice we make out of love.

Jesus says we must be born again. We know about the natural birth. When you are born, you get slapped on the bottom until you cry. That is when you are born naturally into the world, but you are born into the world with a sin nature because of Adam and Eve's disobedience.

ઓC

Behold, I was brought forth in iniquity, and in sin my mother conceived me.

(Psalm 51:5)

So, your spirit needs to be reborn and that is why you invite Jesus to come into your heart. That is when you receive your spiritual birth.

Jesus says in John 3:16:

∽◎૯

For God so loved the world that He gave His only begotten Son, that whoever believes in Him should not perish but have everlasting life.

God is not in love with the world: i.e. the dirt and trees and the plants, although He created them, He is talking about the people in the world. *'He gave His only begotten son that whosoever believes in Him should not perish, but have everlasting life.'*

God said whoever: rich, poor, black, white, prostitute, addict, homosexual or whatever lifestyle you have. God loves everybody, but everybody should make the choice by their own free will to follow Jesus.

∽◎૯

For God did not send His Son into the world to condemn the world, but that the world through Him might be saved.

(John 3:17)

You see, if somebody starts telling you that you are a wicked sinner and a bad person because of what you have done, they are not speaking for God. That is not what God would do. He doesn't want us sinning, but He would not scream at you and judge you. He is going to love you. God desires for you to come into His kingdom. He wants you to know that His great love was so awesome that God sent His only begotten Son, Jesus, to go to the cross of Calvary and He took your place. He died in your place. Jesus went on the cross, took your sins, your sorrow, your pain, your sickness. He did it all for you and therefore it is so important that when you ask Jesus into your heart, you yield yourself to Jesus. It is not by your works. It is much harder to go to hell than to go to heaven. You simply need to receive the gift that was already paid for you when Jesus went to the Cross on your behalf.

Now, some people say to me, *"Well, if God's such a good God, why do people have sicknesses and disease and accidents and why do people die?"*

จଡ୧

For God did not send His Son into the world to condemn the world, but that the world through Him might be saved

(James 1:17)

My reply to them is, *"Well, there are two forces. All the bad is from Satan. All the good things are from God. Stop blaming God for every time something goes wrong. You are blaming the wrong person."*

จଡ୧

The thief does not come except to steal, and to kill, and to destroy. I have come that they may have life, and that they may have it more abundantly.

(John 10:10)

And this is the condemnation, that the light has come into the world, and men loved darkness rather

than light, because their deeds were evil.

(John 3:19)

A lot of times, people don't want anything to do with people talking about Jesus because they are feeling convicted. There is a difference between being judged and feeling conviction. God will let you feel convicted so you will get right with God, because He loves you so much. A father will discipline a child because he knows that if he doesn't discipline his child then they are going to grow up and not have a job and they are not going to do the right thing. The discipline is because of the father's love. God loves us enough to discipline us.

৩৯৫

For whom the LORD loves He chastens, and scourges every son whom He receives."

(Hebrews 12:6)

I will show you how great God's love is.

❧

For when we were still without strength, in due time Christ died for the ungodly. For scarcely for a righteous man will one die; yet perhaps for a good man someone would even dare to die. But God demonstrates His own love toward us, in that while we were still sinners, Christ died for us. Much more then, having now been justified by His blood, we shall be saved from wrath through Him. For if when we were enemies we were reconciled to God through the death of His Son, much more, having been reconciled, we shall be saved by His life. And not only that, but we also rejoice in God through our Lord Jesus Christ, through whom we have now received the reconciliation.

(Romans 5:6-11)

That means He is redeeming us. That means you are being bought, and purchased with the precious blood of Jesus. His blood on the cross of Calvary bought you, but you have to make that choice to say, *'Lord, I accept your blood. I ask you to forgive me of all my sins. I accept your love. I accept your sacrifice. I accept it.'* And then you ask Jesus to come into your heart and take over your life. Surrender your will to Jesus.

You see, we like to be stubborn, saying, *'It is my way or no way.'* It is better to put your hands in the hands of God who created the universe, the stars, the planets and everything that you can see and can't see.

GOD CREATED EVERYTHING!

God said, *"Let there be,"* and everything was created. So, when you put your trust in the hands of God who created everything, how can you go wrong? Let God lead you and guide you and watch over you and protect you because when you do your own thing, you get in trouble and fall off cliffs. Some people wait until they have messed up their life and then they are in jail or something bad has happened to them before they cry out to

God. And then just as soon as everything is good again, they forget God and go back to their old ways again.

❦

For if by the one man's offense death reigned through the one, much more those who receive abundance of grace and of the gift of righteousness will reign in life through the One, Jesus Christ. Therefore, as through one man's offense *judgment came* **to all men, resulting in condemnation, even so through one Man's righteous act** *the free gift came* **to all men, resulting in justification of life. For as by one man's disobedience many were made sinners, so also by one Man's obedience many will be made righteous.**

(Romans 5:17-19)

That is why I started sharing with you and saying, *'You are the righteousness of Christ.'* That is what happened to you when you prayed that prayer, and asked Jesus into your heart; you became righteous. Now, you might not think you are. You might not have changed. You might still have bad habits. But from that moment when you asked Jesus to take over your life, and asked him to lead you, God starts working on you from the inside, working on you to transform you so that is why I said, *'this is your walk with Jesus – your new walk with Jesus.'* That is what this is all about; your new walk with Jesus holding on to your hand.

கௐௐ

For the wages of sin is death, but the gift of God is eternal life in Christ Jesus our Lord.

(Romans 6:23)

God wants us to know that sin will lead to death. Sin will cause your life to be a mess and it will eventually cause you sickness and death. But God says you don't have to experience these, just stop the sinning. You may be saying, *'How do I stop the sinning?'*

You really can't stop sinning on your own. You must put your faith in the total finished work of the cross of Calvary. Ask Jesus to help you stop your bad habits. You should go to God for everything. Only God can help you and change you. Go to God for everything and only through Jesus can you see your life changed. For He says *He will give you abundant life.*

Sin will lead to destruction. Now I am sure nobody wants destruction so just follow Jesus. Follow Jesus in everything you do – let Him be **Big** in you.

Knowing that Christ, having been raised from the dead, dies no more. Death no longer has dominion over Him. For *the death* that He died, He died to sin once for all; but *the life* that He lives, He lives to God. Likewise, you also, reckon yourselves to be dead indeed to sin, but alive to God in Christ

Jesus our Lord. Therefore, do not let sin reign in your mortal body, that you should obey it in its lusts. And do not present your members as instruments of unrighteousness to sin, but present yourselves to God as being alive from the dead, and your members *as* instruments of righteousness to God. ¹⁴ For sin shall not have dominion over you, for you are not under law but under grace.

(Romans 6:9-14)

For the law of the Spirit of life in Christ Jesus has made me free from the law of sin and death.

(Romans 8:2)

So, to present your body means you yield your body to the Lord. There are only two things you must do to receive Jesus. It is very simple.

❦

That if you confess with your mouth the Lord Jesus and believe in your heart that God has raised Him from the dead, you will be saved.

(Romans 10:9)

What are you being saved from? He says you are going to be saved. Well, if you are going to be saved, you must be saved from something. If a little child runs out into the road after a ball and I am a grownup and I run and grab the child just before a car runs over him/her and I pull them to safety, I have saved that child. God is saving us from hell; He is saving us from destruction, sickness and disease. He wants to bless us so He is saving us from terrible things, from the wrath and from hell, so we need to ask Jesus into our hearts. That is what He is saving you from.

❦

For with the heart one believes unto righteousness, and with the mouth confession is made unto salvation.

For the Scripture says, "Whoever believes on Him will not be put to shame."

(Romans 10:10-11)

So many people say, *'Well, I don't know if I want to be a Christian. If I read my bible and pray, people will make fun of me.'*

The bible says you won't be put to shame so get that out of your head. You will not be put to shame.

ﻌﻬﻌ

For "whoever calls on the name of the LORD shall be saved."

(Romans 10:13)

So, a lot of times people repeat a long prayer. Praying is good. But the truth of the matter is, you could be praying anywhere at any time – you don't have to be in a church because it is not a church relationship. It is a relationship between you and God, you and Jesus Christ. Jesus Christ connects you to the Father. You just call out to Jesus.

The Bible says, if you call on the name of the Lord you can be saved. Let's not make it so hard. Somebody could just be saying, *'Jesus, Jesus, You are my Lord!'* and they are saved. They called out to Jesus, *'You are my Lord, my saviour'*, then they must believe He died on the cross for our sins and He, Jesus, took our place on the cross. When we ask Jesus to forgive us of all our sins, and we mean it with all our heart, we are saved. A lot of people can call out to the Lord, but they don't believe it in their heart so there are two things that are requirements; one is the heart issue – what is in your heart. You could pray prayers; you could say a bunch of words, but if it is not in your heart, it doesn't mean anything. It is when your heart connects with the words you are saying – your heart, your mind, your body, your emotions, everything says, *'I believe that Jesus died. I believe Jesus took my place. I believe Jesus redeemed me from the fall in the garden. Jesus restored me. Jesus cleansed me. Jesus washed me.'* Without the shedding of the blood, there is no remission of sin. Jesus is the one who paid the price for us to be cleansed. So, all you should do is believe and receive – very simple. It is an act of your faith. Ask God to forgive you of all your sins, and believe that Jesus has paid the price for you on the cross.

If you have never asked Jesus into your heart, let's pray it now:

'Dear Jesus, I know I am a sinner. I am sorry for my sins. I repent of my ways and of my sins. Help me not to sin anymore. I ask you dear Jesus, come into my heart, be my Lord, be my saviour. I will follow you, love you and serve you all the days of my life. Thank you, Jesus, for saving my soul!'

If you just prayed that prayer, there are a few things you need to do. First, go **confess** this to somebody – tell a relative, get on the phone, call somebody and say, *'I just prayed and asked Jesus into my heart.'* Confess it to somebody.

Secondly, you need to **pray**. What is prayer? Maybe you don't know what prayer is. Prayer is you talking to God. And some people say, *'Well, how do I pray? What kind of prayer do I pray?'*

You know how to talk to a friend, don't you? You know how to talk to your spouse? You just talk – just talk. Just sit in a quiet place, and if you want to talk out loud, just make sure there are no people looking at you thinking you are crazy, but just start talking to God. Just speak to Him just like you would talk to anybody else. He is always listening. So, that is called prayer.

The next thing you need to do is get in the **Word**. Now, If I held a brand-new baby that was just born in my arms and don't give him/her any milk to drink, the baby will die. So, you just had a born-again experience – remember that I said your spirit would be born again. So now that you have had this born-again experience, you must give food to this body. So, you need food to eat to give nourishment to your body. Likewise, you need spiritual food for your spirit and soul, and that is the Word of God. So, you should start studying the Word of God.

And the third thing is find a **good church** where they only preach the Bible. Find a good Spirit-filled church.

The fourth thing you need to do is so important. You need the baptism of the Holy Spirit.

THE BAPTISM IN THE HOLY SPIRIT

Now that you have received Jesus as your Lord and Saviour, what is the next step that you need to live a strong Christian life.

The next thing you need is what Jesus said to his disciple, *"Don't go do anything until you receive power" (Luke 24:49)*. I want to explain to you how to have the power to overcome sin; how to have the power to walk a victorious life; by receiving the in-filling of the Holy Spirit. The same Holy Spirit who was working in Jesus, doing miracles through Jesus, is the same Holy Spirit who wants to come and live inside of you.

Before Jesus ascended to heaven, He explained to His Apostles that they needed to wait for the infilling of the Holy Spirit.

And being assembled together with *them*, He commanded them not to depart from Jerusalem, but to wait for the Promise of the Father, "which," *He said*, "you have heard

from Me; for John truly baptized with water, but you shall be baptized with the Holy Spirit not many days from now."

(Acts 1:4-5)

They waited in the upper room - there were a lot of people in that upper room – 120 – both men and women. Mary, the mother of Jesus was there, the other Mary was there, other women was there, so this was men and women gathered in one place waiting to receive the infilling of the Holy Spirit and they were gloriously filled with the Holy Spirit that day. That was the day of Pentecost.

Over my years of ministry, I have seen so many filled with the Holy Spirit. Even children of all ages, gloriously filled and used in the gifts of the Holy Spirit.

∞∞

But you shall receive power when the Holy Spirit has come upon you; and you shall be witnesses to Me in Jerusalem, and in all Judea

**and Samaria, and to the end of the
earth."**

(Acts 1:8)

The word 'power' in this scripture means 'dunamis.'
Dunamis means dynamite, which is the dynamite
power that can blow up mountains. That is the
kind of power that God has placed inside you.
The Holy Spirit will make you a powerful witness
and help you. The Holy Spirit will be a teacher, a
comforter, a guide and will encourage you, direct
you and be with you.

෧෧෧

**When the Day of Pentecost had
fully come, they were all with one
accord in one place. And suddenly
there came a sound from heaven,
as of a rushing mighty wind, and it
filled the whole house where they
were sitting. Then there appeared
to them divided tongues, as of fire,
and *one* sat upon each of them. And
they were all filled with the Holy**

Spirit and began to speak with other tongues, as the Spirit gave them utterance.

(Acts 2:1-4)

The Holy Spirit will come and live inside you and the Holy Spirit will talk to God, not in English or Spanish or French, but will speak in a heavenly language.

Paul wrote under the inspiration of God:

∽ළ

Though I speak with the tongues of men and of angels, but have not love, I have become sounding brass or a clanging cymbal.

(1 Corinthians 13:1)

When we speak in the tongues of men, somebody is going to understand it. If I speak Chinese, the Chinese can understand it; if I speak Korean, the Koreans are going to understand it; if I speak English, those who speak English will understand it. When we are filled with the Holy Spirit, this unknown language, your prayer language, will come gushing out of us. No one will understand it without divine interpretation. It is a language we don't understand, but God understands it and angels understand it. When we speak in this unknown language, angels go on assignment and it builds us up. We won't understand it. God wants you to have every gift He has given to His children and He wants you to have the infilling of the Holy Spirit.

❧

Pursue love, and desire spiritual *gifts*, but especially that you may prophesy. For he who speaks in a tongue does not speak to men but to God, for no one understands *him*; however, in the spirit he speaks mysteries.

(1 Corinthians 14:1-2)

You are speaking things you don't know. And the Bible says no one understands it so that means you won't understand it either.

A lot of people will say, *"Well, why would I pray with this language that I don't understand?"*

You might not understand it, but God's doing great mysteries and working things out on your behalf and maybe moving things out of the way in your life – maybe taking stuff that is junk in your life out of you and setting you free. God is building you up. So, we don't understand all the mysteries of God, but just receive it because He told his early church, *"Don't do anything 'til you receive this gift."*

If Jesus told His disciples not to do anything back in those days, well, right now, in the days that we are living in, we need it more than ever, because the world is getting worst and we need to walk in God's power.

ഏര

For if I pray in a tongue, my spirit prays, but my understanding is unfruitful.

(1 Corinthians 14:14)

When we are praying in tongues, we don't understand a word of what we are saying, but we know it is fruitful because we see the fruit. You don't understand this language that you are speaking, but it will just come out of you; an unknown language and you should pray in this unknown language as often as you can; the more, the better.

In Acts chapter 10, Peter was having a vision. The Lord tells him to go to a household and teach them the Word of God. Peter goes to Cornelius' house and there was a whole group of people there. Peter preaches to them the Word of God.

∾✿∽

While Peter was still speaking these words, the Holy Spirit fell upon all those who heard the word. And those of the circumcision who believed were astonished, as many as came with Peter, because the gift of the Holy Spirit had been poured out on the Gentiles also. For they heard them speak with tongues and magnify God.

(Acts 10:44-47)

The people of the household, who were uncircumcised Gentiles, suddenly started speaking in these unknown languages.

The only requirement to receive the baptism of the Holy Spirit is to be saved (born again) and desire to be filled with the Holy spirit, then pray and ask the Father to fill you with the Holy Spirit, then Jesus will baptise you with the Holy Spirit. That is all there is to it.

In Acts 19, Paul is travelling from place to place and he comes up on some believers. There are 12 men.

∽ॐ৹

He said to them, "Did you receive the Holy Spirit when you believed?" So they said to him, "We have not so much as heard whether there is a Holy Spirit." And he said to them, "Into what then were you baptized?" So they said, "Into John's baptism." Then Paul said, "John indeed baptized with

a baptism of repentance, saying to the people that they should believe on Him who would come after him, that is, on Christ Jesus." When they heard *this*, they were baptized in the name of the Lord Jesus.

(Acts 19:2-5)

So, they were baptized. And then it said, *'And when Paul had laid hands on them, the Holy Spirit came upon them and they spoke with tongues and prophesied. And the men were about 12 in all.'*

So everywhere Paul went, people started to get filled with the Holy Spirit. Everywhere Peter went, people started to get filled with the Holy Spirit. The early church was getting filled with the Holy Spirit and the church was growing because it is not by might, or by our power but by the Spirit of God. We are spirit beings and God wants us to worship in spirit and truth and He wants us to pray in the spirit. When we are praying in the spirit in this unknown language, then we are having direct communication to God. It is a direct line to God Almighty, and we don't always understand it. God doesn't always let us know what we are saying and what is happening.

∞❧

I indeed baptize you with water unto repentance, but He who is coming after me is mightier than I, whose sandals I am not worthy to carry. He will baptize you with the Holy Spirit and fire.

(Matthew 3:11)

Baptism with water unto repentance is a different baptism. That is when people get down in the water and get baptized in the water, but baptism of the Holy Spirit is a different baptism when the Holy Spirit comes and lives inside you.

∞❧

His winnowing fan is in His hand, and He will thoroughly clean out His threshing floor, and gather His wheat into the barn; but He will burn up the chaff with unquenchable fire."

(Matthew 3:12)

The reason you need to have the infilling of the Holy Spirit – the baptism of the Holy Spirit – is the Holy Spirit will go inside you and start cleansing you from the inside out and doing a mighty work so you are ready for heaven. You see, the Holy Spirit is the Helper to help us do what God's plans and desires are for our lives. He is the Guarantee to keep us on course. Jesus comes and He purchases you and then the Holy Spirit is a guarantee to make sure you stay on course. If you start getting off course, the Holy Spirit will correct you. So, you will learn to hear and recognize the Holy Spirit and His voice.

Some churches and denominations will tell you the Holy Spirit is of the devil. That is a lie from the pit of hell and I am going to prove it to you. In Luke 11, Jesus is talking about prayer.

ॐ

"So I say to you, ask, and it will be given to you; seek, and you will find; knock, and it will be opened to you. For everyone who asks receives, and he who seeks finds, and to him who knocks it will be

opened. If a son asks for bread from any father among you, will he give him a stone? Or if *he asks* for a fish, will he give him a serpent instead of a fish? Or if he asks for an egg, will he offer him a scorpion? If you then, being evil, know how to give good gifts to your children, how much more will *your* heavenly Father give the Holy Spirit to those who ask Him!"

(Luke 11:9-13)

Jesus is saying this Holy Spirit that He will give you will dwell inside of you and will be strength to you. He is not going to give you something bad. He will give you something that will encourage you, build you up and strengthen you.

ॐ

"If you love Me, keep My commandments. And I will pray the Father, and He will give you another Helper, that He may abide with you forever— the Spirit of truth, whom the world cannot receive, because it neither sees Him nor knows Him; but you know Him, for He dwells with you and will be in you. I will not leave you orphans; I will come to you. "A little while longer and the world will see Me no more, but you will see Me. Because I live, you will live also. At that day, you will know that I *am* in My Father, and you in Me, and I in you. He who has My commandments and keeps them, It Is he who loves Me. And he who loves Me will be loved by My Father, and I will love him and manifest Myself to him."

(John 14:15-21)

ಞಲ

"These things I have spoken to you while being present with you. But the Helper, the Holy Spirit, whom

the Father will send in My name, He will teach you all things, and bring to your remembrance all things that I said to you. Peace I leave with you, My peace I give to you; not as the world gives do I give to you. Let not your heart be troubled, neither let it be afraid.

(John 14:25-27)

Please note that when the Bible mentions 'spirit' with a lower-case 's' it means your spirit, but with the capital 'S' it means God's Spirit.

God is going to give you the Holy Spirit to walk with you, to talk with you, to help you, to always be there for you. He wants you to know that the Holy Spirit will be there for you always.

The Holy Spirit is the third person of the Godhead, which is called the Trinity: The Father, Son (Jesus Christ), and Holy Spirit (Holy Ghost) all working together as a unit to bless your life.

✵

For there are three that bear witness in heaven: the Father, the Word, and the Holy Spirit; and these three are one.

(1 John 5:7)

The Word is Jesus. The Third person of the Godhead, the Holy Spirit, wants to come and live inside you.

✵

But you, beloved, building yourselves up on your most holy faith, praying in the Holy Spirit, keep yourselves in the love of God, looking for the mercy of our Lord Jesus Christ unto eternal life.

(Jude 20-21)

God is saying the more you pray in the Holy Spirit, the stronger you will be.

ॐ

"I still have many things to say to you, but you cannot bear *them* now. However, when He, the Spirit of truth, has come, He will guide you into all truth; for He will not speak on His own *authority*, but whatever He hears He will speak; and He will tell you things to come. He will glorify Me, for He will take of what is Mine and declare *it* to you. All things that the Father has are Mine. Therefore I said that He will take of Mine and declare *it* to you.

(John 16:12-15)

Jesus was explaining to His Disciples that He was leaving, and He was going to send the Third person of the Godhead, the Holy Spirit, to them to be with them (and you) always.

God wants us to pray in the Holy Spirit always and fill ourselves up. He wants you and I to build ourselves up by praying in the Holy Ghost.

I know you may not understand this, but everything must come by faith. If Jesus told His disciples not to go anywhere until they receive this gift, then you want to make sure you have everything that God has for you. I am sure you don't want to limit the things you could do. I don't know about you, but I am one of those people who says, *'Whatever you have for me God, I want it. Bring it on!'*

Do you want everything that God has for you? Of course, the greatest gift is salvation, when you ask Jesus into your heart. That was the greatest thing that could ever happen to you. Jesus has much more for you and Jesus said:

∽ର

Nevertheless I tell you the truth. It is to your advantage that I go away; for if I do not go away, the Helper will not come to you; but if I depart, I will send Him to you.

(John 16:7)

The Comforter or Helper in the scriptures is another name for the Holy Spirit.

I would like to explain it this way. It is like a rocket taking off from Cape Canaveral. The rocket goes up in the air and it blasts off and goes way up into space. To get far, it must have a booster. And then a second booster kicks in, and sends that rocket into warp speed and into outer space. Likewise, the Holy Spirit is here to take you into that power source after you receive Jesus, the greatest gift. The Holy Spirit will empower you to walk with God.

Now, you know how cell-phones work or how electricity works. If you don't plug your cell-phone into a power source and you just let your battery run down, soon your cell-phone will not work. Every now and again, you need to plug your phone into a power source. Sometimes, when I get tired, I start praying in tongues, and Holy Spirit energizes and starts using me to know things about people supernaturally. You need to plug into the power source of the Holy Ghost and keep your spirit built up. God says you will be led by the spirit of God.

ొౖౖౖౖ

For as many as are led by the Spirit of God, these are sons of God.
(Romans 8:14)

Steps to Baptism in the Holy Spirit

1. **The Holy Spirit is the source of a powerful Life.**

   a. **Acts 1:8.** "Power" and abundant strength and ability to be an overcomer and live a victorious life.

   b. **John 14:26.** Comforter and teacher, who helps you in your everyday life situations.

   c. **Acts 19:1-2,5-6.** Baptism of the Holy Spirit is a separate experience from the work of the Holy Spirit in conversion.

   d. **Acts 10:44-46.** People were filled with the Holy Spirit and spoke in tongues.

2. **What happens when you are filled with the Holy Spirit?**

Acts 2:4

> And they were all filled with the Holy Spirit and began to speak with other tongues, as the Spirit gave them utterance.

The Holy Spirit is already here for every born-again person. You do not need to wait for Him. Just ask to receive the Holy Spirit.

Acts 2:38-39

> Then Peter said to them, "Repent, and let every one of you be baptized in the name of Jesus Christ for the remission of sins; and you shall receive the gift of the Holy Spirit. "For the promise is to you and to your children, and to all who are afar off, as many as the Lord our God will call."

3. **Your mind won't understand or gain anything from speaking in tongues.** (It will sound useless and foolish). You are speaking mysteries to God, not to man.

1 Corinthians 14:2

For he who speaks in a tongue does not speak to men but to God, for no one understands him; however, in the spirit he speaks mysteries.

1 Corinthians 14:14-15

For if I pray in a tongue, my spirit prays, but my understanding is unfruitful. What is the conclusion then? I will pray with the spirit, and I will also pray with the understanding. I will sing with the spirit, and I will also sing with the understanding.

Speaking in tongues is an act of your will. God will not force you to do it, or do it for you.

4. **If you ask for the Holy Spirit in faith, you will receive Him.**

Luke 11:13

"If you then, being evil, know how to give good gifts to your children, how much more will your Heavenly Father give the Holy Spirit to those who seek Him."

5. **Are you ready to receive the Holy Spirit now?** Now, pray and have faith in your heart and invite the Holy Spirit to fill you.

6. **Pray this prayer now and activate your faith.** Let God use your mouth to speak in a new language, and let the Holy Spirit take total control of your life.

7. **Now pray this prayer:** "*Father*, I am asking you for the gift of the Holy Spirit. Jesus, baptize me with the Holy Spirit and fire. *Dear Holy Spirit*, come into me and fill me."

   Boldly speak out in other tongues. Let the Holy Spirit just fill your mouth and use you.

Now that you have Jesus in your heart and are filled with the Holy Spirit, find a wonderful church to start attending and growing, and being nurtured. Start reading/studying your Bible and spend time in the Word of God each day. Pray in tongues every day and then you will start walking in the realm of the miraculous with your new walk with Christ Jesus.

Now that you have received Jesus inside you and you now have Him in your heart, Jesus is now inviting you to know God the Father.

God the Father and Jesus Christ have introduced you to the Holy Spirit now living inside of you. So now, go in the power of God, in the power of the Father, Son and Holy Spirit now working in your life. There are many other gifts that God will use you to walk in.

Our prayer for you:

"Father in heaven, we pray that you will strengthen and make Your word so powerful and real to them. Give them Your revelation knowledge. Help them to pray in the Holy Spirit. Direct them, lead them, and help them to find a good strong church and to grow in the strength and knowledge of Your love. Your power will become so very clear, empower them, have them stay in Your Word, direct them. As You have begun this great work inside of them, continue and let them have a wonderful walk with Jesus, amen."

You can visit our website at
www.joanpearce.org for other tools and
resources to help you grow.

*Please send your reviews, testimonials and
questions to:*

**Channel of Love Ministries
P. O. Box 20069
Bradenton, FL 34204**

Made in the USA
Middletown, DE
05 January 2023